BE THE BRAND: The Ultimate Guide to Building Your Personal Brand

Jules Marcoux © All Rights reserved.

Check out my website and blog for free tips and to learn more about the marketing services I offer.

www.julesmarcoux.com

Introduction

Jules Marcoux? Who the hell is that?

That's actually a great question, but in all honesty, I'm a nobody.

I grew up in a quiet suburb of cold Quebec City. But unlike the smallness of where I lived, my dreams and creativity were bigger than the confines of where I lived. Since an early age, my creativity ran rampant and was constantly on the search for the next thing to do. From fluttering tunes of music, to lifelike portraits, to photography of the world that was constantly changing round me, I created.

And though my creative mind was expansive, my story is but a short one.

At the age of 16 years old, I started to seriously invest myself into one of my lifelong passions: music. With the few but hard earned dollars saved up in my piggy bank, I bought serious studio and video equipment to help me actualize my lifelong dream: to become a rap star. I know, it may be a funny dream to have, but it was something I was completely serious about.

Fast forward 2 years later, I was on stage at one the biggest venues in Quebec, actualizing my dream and displaying my talent through a passion that I really invested time into. And what was so great about all of this success? Girls were asking for my photo in shopping malls. Photos!? Who would've guessed that a small time kid would start getting fans who randomly tried to get a quick pic. But hey, I wasn't complaining. If you're interested in learning more of my rapping days, just search "Jaymark" on YouTube, otherwise let's get on with this story.

While displaying my passion of rap I wanted something more, but I wasn't sure what that something was. Was it more money? Maybe. Entertainment and fun? Perhaps. Fame and recognition? Most likely. So to meet these ends I started to throw nightclub events. Then pool parties. Then back to more nightclub events. And so on. This back and forth soon started catching crowds of people from just 10 people to over 4,000.

But I soon lost interest in all of that.

I quickly began to wonder: where did the creative kid go?

I knew I could do more. I knew I could *be* more.

I read numerous books regarding marketing, and my short music career and nightclub business – which was pretty successful for a young guy like me – taught me a lot about the ever elusive yet oh so interesting realm of marketing.

But what could I do with that? What was the next step for me and my supposedly learned marketing knowledge?

Well, I started to invest my creativity into bigger projects. Through a string of events and perhaps even lady luck being on my side, I found a couple of clients that had immense faith in me and in my services, and then it grew from there.

I now get the chance to work on projects with clients and brands of all shapes and size; whether it is helping the local coffee shop, or putting my skills to the profit of bigger brands.

Last year, in 2015, I decided that I would write my first book, an enormous project for anyone. Needless to say, I was both ecstatic and completely unprepared to take on such a feat. I mean, yes, I'm good at marketing and yes,I delivered massively favorable results to clients. But I didn't work 20 years in the marketing industry, I never sold a business to Apple, and I never really had a successful venture that would traditionally classify me as a huge business tycoon.

But I said screw it, and I wrote the god damned book, not because I just wanted a book under my name, but because my passions led me there. And that passion not only led to a finished book, but made it a best-seller on Amazon.

As of today (2016), more than 250,000 people are following my journey and sharing their passion of marketing with me. I get to work on great projects and with even greater individuals, and I get to run my own solo marketing agency.

I can say with conviction that there is at least one person from every corner of the world learning from my vision on marketing. And yes, that was probably the most obvious brag out there, but hey, for a guy who wasn't classified as a traditional marketing tycoon, I was proud in achieving such a great goal.

I literally started from nothing and now people stop me in small town Chipotles to tell me how I inspired them, even when I'm 2,000 miles from home. That's insane, mind-boggling, and I absolutely love it.

I'm so immensely proud that every day around the world, people trust the Jules Marcoux brand, are learning from it, and are venturing out to pursue their own endeavors and dreams by looking to my brand as a source of inspiration and motivation. It's both scary at times but just as exciting to have people look up to you in such a big way.

So, What Is This Book About?

See how I ended the last few sentences by writing "the Jules Marcoux brand"?

That's because I've always considered *myself* as the brand.

The very first years of my consulting business has been a constant struggle regarding whether I should create a completely different brand from my personal brand for my business.

Then, after thousands of hours of anxiety, research, and plain old reading books, I came to a realization: People don't buy from businesses; they buy from *people*. Indeed, even if they love a specific company, they decide to do business with it more times than not because of the people behind it, the individuals who endorse or represent the ideals of the brand.

So I asked myself: instead of focusing my energy on building a completely separate brand, why don't I brand myself and make *myself* a business?

So that's what I've decided to do since the last 7 years. And frankly, this has been one of the best decisions I have ever made. My journey has involved a constant hustle, and a constant strive towards bettering myself, my brand, and the relations I have with those around me. In doing so, I am able to grow my personal brand and shape it the way that I want it to be.

And this book is about just that.

It is not a book on business nor a book on how to get rich quick or successful overnight.

In no way in hell am I the best business man or the richest person to come to advice for.

I'm just a young marketer servicing businesses around the world and having fun building projects. Beyond that, I'm a guy who tries to think as differently as possible from the conventional wisdom that so many people follow in hopes of creating my own path that other people can follow too.

If you want to learn how you can leverage and grow your personal brand, you picked up the right book. This book is a collection of short lessons – because I've learned that simplicity is key and – on ways to build the foundations of your personal brand, methods to growing your tribe, tips on monetizing your personal brand, and how to reinvent yourself constantly to be more in tune with your mission and your vision.

I sincerely hope you enjoy this journey and I am confident there is something for everyone found within the pages of this book.

What Is A Personal Brand And Why Should I Build One?

Personal branding and its power is structured around this very simple principle: the more you market yourself and treat yourself like a brand, the more successful you will be. Personal branding means building your reputation, growing your following, and constructing your name.

It also means leveraging it and effectively using it to make capital.

Let me ask you this: what does Oprah, Richard Branson, Steve Jobs, Picasso, David Ogilvy, and Michael Jordan have in common? They all treated themselves as brands to get where they are today.

Now I know what you're thinking! "But they are celebrities! And they are rich and famous!" Though this is true, it was ultimately their personal branding and marketing that got them them where they are not the other way around. And the good news is that your personal brand can, and should, be built very early in your career. You're never too young, too old, too unpopular, too whatever to piece it together.

You might also be thinking: "They are just so talented, it's not about marketing!" Are you sure? How many people are great and never get discovered? How many people sing better than Justin Bieber but still live in their parents' basement? Unfortunately, the number is much too great to even fathom.

That's why I love to say that marketing always wins. You can't beat it. Even the best talent will never beat a well marketed one. Of course I'm not saying that talent is useless, but talent that is supplemented by marketing leads to attention and therefore eventual success.

A well built personal brand will result in a number of things: better business opportunities, more job offers, increased clientele, greater revenue, more companies asking you to endorse their products, and even better treatment when you go to your local restaurant. And no, that last one is not a joke.

I believe every single person in this world should strive to work on their personal brand. Your business can fail. A project can fail. But your brand will stay if created effectively and with time and effort.

Part 1 – The Foundations

What Are You Known For? You Have To Own A Niche.

When building your personal brand, the number one question to ask yourself is: what do I want to be known for?

Think of any celebrity, artist, or entrepreneur; and you'll soon realize that they are known for something in particular. It may be a talent, an achievement, a discipline, an expertise, a style of work, or a way of thinking. And be very careful, we're not talking about style or anything superficial. We're talking about the craft or anything that makes an individual stand out from the crowd.

Here's a quote by Robin Sharma that I enjoy reading once in a while: "My work is my art, and my art is my life."

This is powerful. There are so many influencers out there on social media that have many followers, but no craft and are quick to become yesterday's news rather than innovators who stay relevant regardless of the times. Personal branding is much more about being recognized for your craft and followers comes afterwards.

Personal branding is not about how many people know about you. Personal branding is about how many people know you for what you really are.

So here it is: what is the #1 thing you want to be known for? Finding this out is one of the most important steps in actualizing your brand and your image.

Who Do You Want To Be Known By?

Have you ever tried to sell dog food to a cat? It's not easy.

You can't try to please everyone and you certainly can't get everyone to get behind your brand.

Therefore, personal branding is about focusing your energy on building a relationship with people who matter, people who will enjoy to be in your circle and are open to what you have to offer.

Take a sheet of paper right away and write down who you aim to be known by. By defining your target audience, you can more easily build a brand that is both tailored to the interests of that audience, but also able to incorporate your own talents, passions, and interests into the brand and the content that the brand hopes to push out.

Your Vision Has To Be Crystal Clear

Feel like talking about clarity? Let's go.

If you're building your personal brand, your vision has to be crystal clear.

Now you may ask yourself: what is a vision? A vision is simply picturing yourself in 20 years and envision where you will be, who you want to be, and most importantly, what you will be doing?

As a personal brand, you have to be in it for the long term. You have to stop getting distracted by everything and work according to your vision. Once you've done that, work backwards.

A lot of people won't get behind your vision and some may even try to completely prevent you from achieving your goals.

However, you have to be the one making the moves towards your aspirations and follow the path that you have laid out infant of you, regardless of what others may do or think.

And most importantly, every single step you make should be purposeful, meaningful, and bring you closer to your goal.

Focus On Your Strengths

A lot of people invest too much energy on trying to improve their weaknesses, instead of capitalizing on their strengths. By doing this, these individuals simply jump from being mediocre to being average, rather than heading towards greatness.

And building a personal brand is simply working towards becoming the best of the best. Branding needs influence. Influence comes in part from authority. Authority comes from being seen as the greatest at something.

When you focus on your strengths, you can – with smart work – get from good to great at your craft.

Find what your native strengths, your inner talents are, and focus on those aspects and really cultivate them to the peak of their heights.

Become the greatest at what you're already great.

Focus On Your Flaws

Ironically, building your personal brand is also about focusing on your flaws. It's about being authentic and honest about your imperfections. If you try to hide things from your audience – or if you try to build a perfect image of yourself – they will know it and it won't work. The key to many companies' successes is being as transparent as possible and respecting your audience's intelligence.

Of course, many people point out that I never went to college. I never sold a company to Apple. I've actually never worked in the "marketing world" as an entry level job. But though I never did these things, I learned the law of the land by doing my own projects and being a freelancer since the beginning.

And I'm embracing that. Some people hate it but for others, even this experience is meaningful.

For example, a lot of new entrepreneurs building their first businesses would try to brand themselves as "Entrepreneur" or as "Serial Entrepreneur." And sadly, that's wrong. You shouldn't do that.

Instead, if you're building your first clothing brand, the best way is to actually brand yourself is as someone building their first clothing brand. Want to brag? Want to make it bigger? Brand yourself as someone on its way to building a billion-dollar brand.

Are you a math teacher who quit his or job to open a new restaurant? Brand yourself as that, as there aren't many people who would fit your category. Needless to say, your uniqueness and your story is an advantage and is what sets you apart from the rest.

Ask yourself: what am I really? What am I really doing right now? What is my true story?

Never try to brand yourself as something you're not. Instead, focus on who you really are, focus on telling the world your real story, and brand yourself like it. And trust me, your audience will be much more open to your brand.

What's The Visual Style?

Every great brand has its own visual style.

Apple? Simplicity, minimalism, and black and white. Red Bull? Red and blue and lots of colors.

But it's not much different for personal brands. Steve Jobs? Turtle neck. Danielle Laporte? White backgrounds with handwritten lettering. Tony Robbins? Blue color. Seth Godin? His photo and the orange color.

When building the foundations of your personal brand, you have to decide what the visual style will be. You have to decide what makes you unique visually, and to leverage it.

Invest In Great Photos

Invest in professional photos as they are a great way to show the world who you are. It's also a great way to communicate your true self.

Social media is giving us the opportunity to connect with a lot of people and to build an audience bigger than ever. Investing in photos that represent who you are will show people that you're professional and take your craft seriously. It will also communicate the quality of your personal brand.

Let me ask you this: if you go to a restaurant, do you expect the menu to have crappy photos of their food? No. Why should it be any different for your personal brand? If you're trying to sell your brand, you also have to take time in selling yourself.

I set up meetings with photographers at least once a month. I can later use these photos on my social pages, on my website, on my promotional flyers, on my proposal, or anything related to my personal brand.

It's a great way to show who I am. It's a great way to position myself as an expert.

Again, invest in great photos.

Build Your Website, Now

If you're reading this book right now and aim to build your personal brand, you should absolutely go buy the domain name for your name or your nickname.

Once this is done, it's time to build your website. I normally advise people to set up a blog. There are tons of solutions available nowadays to help you build it at a very affordable price.

Your website is the root of your online presence. This is where people will be able to read your story and see what you're working on. This is where you'll be able to share and showcase your expertise. It can also be a place for you to sell products and monetize your personal brand. This is where you will be able to collect leads and have your audience and prospects get in touch with you. When people Google you, they will end up there. Therefore, it's important to take some time when designing and filling your site with exemplary content that will give a good impression.

Should You Have A Nickname?

You can either build your personal brand under your own name, or under a nickname. Let me give you an example.

Let's say that your name is Bob Doe and you love beer. You could either build your brand around your name, or around a nickname such as "Bob Beer" or "Bob Loves Beer".

Or let's say that your family name is Bernitckandios. Bob Bernitckandios to be exact. One idea would be to brand yourself under the alias "Bob Bern," which would make it much easier for people to remember you and pronounce your name. Of course there is nothing wrong with doing this as its a means of making your name and thus your brand a success.

Choosing the right scenario depends on your industry and the vision that you have for your brand. But you have to choose carefully; choosing a nickname that is too focused on a specific subject, or a specific industry, won't leave you much room for flexibility.

Let's Make A Logo

Once you have decided to either go with your name or with a nick name, it's time to design your logo. Just as a normal brand, you need one that stands out but is also symbolic of your overall brand and the type of mood you want to give off. In this respect, the logo can be as simple or as intricate as you want long as it fits in with the overall concept and ideals of your brand. A nice rule of thumb is that simple logos normally work better when starting out, as it's easy to miss the mark when pushing for a more complex logo.

Your logo should be simple, versatile, timeless, and meaningful.

Have Social Pages

Social media is indeed the best way to build an audience as its reach is global and connecting is as easy as a few clicks.

The number one step in building your audience there is to be present on social media such as Twitter, Facebook, Instagram, Periscope; the list goes on. Go ahead and set up your pages if it's not done yet. Polish your bio and find a main goal for each platform. Every social media is different and they should be treated as so.

One more thing. As things change so fast these days, I believe you should be fast and reserve usernames as soon you hear a new platform is launched. It will help you control your presence on social media. You have to jump on there early.

If You're Going To Have A Business Card, Make It Right

I never had a business card as they always seemed to be a waste of paper and time. The truth of the matter is that if people really need to reach me, they'll know how without having to resort to a business card. In today's social media age, business cards really are obsolete as personal branding can and will ensure that the right people will be able to contact me with no trouble.

People that put too much focus on the importance of the business card normally forget the importance of building relations. If you have my email, or phone number, it means there's a reason for that and that we have built a relation prior to that exchange. On the other hand, a business card is often times just given out and that's it; not much conversation or effort is put in for that exchange to take place.

Now, even though I'm not a big fan, a business card can be helpful in *some* instances and in some industries. But if you're going to utilize this, you have to stand out and make sure your card has something eye-popping.

I know someone who goes to trade-shows all year long and always comes back with a pocketful of business cards. He almost throws them all in the trash bin. Except the ones that stand out and of course those from people who took the time to build some form of relationship.

There's a multitude of ways you can stand out with your business card. You can play with shapes, colors, words, and many other things. You can also have a "v-card" which is a virtual card.

In my instance, when I really want someone to remember me and I want to leave them with something that stands out, I leave them one of my books and sign my contact information on the first page. Every time I do it, I'm hearing back from these people. It's more expensive than a business card, but it's worth the investment and is definitely something different.

That leaves us on an idea. Maybe your business card isn't a business card. Maybe it's your book. Maybe it's a piece of your clothing brand. Maybe it's a drawing from you.

Leave people something that stands out and has some meaning behind it.

Part 2 – The Come Up

"Everyone wants to live on top of the mountain, but all the happiness and growth occurs while you're climbing it." — Andy Rooney

It's Not About How Perfect Your Story Is – It's About Telling It In An Immersive Way

In the first part of this book, I talk about how you should embrace your flaws in a relevant way. While you grow your personal brand, it is always important to stay true to this rule. You have to stay true to your story.

The beauty of this concept lies in one simple principle: nobody has your story and nobody can tell it the way you can.

That being said, growing your personal brand is all about telling your story to the world while you're writing it.

In my case, I didn't wait to be the most successful marketer in the world to share my story. I've actually decided to share my story while I'm in the process of creating myself.

I believe that building your personal brand is all about that: staying true to your story and telling it while you're writing it.

And so It's time to write.

You Don't Have To Produce Content On Every Channel

In theory you could, but you don't want to. A lot of people do this wrong. They think that having an account and posting on every social platform is a strategy, while it isn't.

By trying to be active on every social media, you dilute your efforts and rather than becoming exceptional on one social media, you're mediocre at best on a multitude of social media.

When building a brand – and a personal brand – I advise people to focus on a maximum of 4 social channels, with one that is the main pillar of their strategy. This way, your content is not being spread out to the point of not being relevant, but spread tut enough to interact with a a great number of people.

Never Drive While Your Eyes Are Closed

Have you ever tried to drive with your eyes closed? Trust me, you don't want to.

Just like when you drive a car, you need to keep your eyes open and be ready to take in information when marketing a brand. Part of this information intake comes from being obsessed with data, analytics, metrics, and research. These things are the root of your strategy. What you can't track, you can't improve. What you can't learn, you can't implement.

By keeping your eyes open on these things, you improve your chances of taking great decisions while building your personal brands.

It not only helps you set goals, but it will help you to know what you should be doing, what you shouldn't be doing and what to improve. Too many people are trying to market their brand – or personal brand – without even knowing when, where, how and who is buying their products or services.

There are a lot of analytics and data gathering solutions at your reach, for very little or no cost. Google Analytics, Iconosquare, Mailchimp reports, Adwords and Facebook ads reports, Buffer, Sumome, Flurry, and so many more. It's all about knowing which one is best for you and the industry your in.

While analytics and data will guide your decisions, research and learning will help you know what are your possibilities.

In my instance, I am subscribed to around 25 newsfeeds about marketing. I set up Google alerts on consumer trends and on news in the marketing industry. I read papers and university researches about consumer psychology and marketing. I also constantly read and listen to what my customers and audience say. They are the one I need to serve.

Become obsessed with analytics and research, you'll start noticing trends and opportunities and you'll take better decisions. They are your most loyal customers and they consume and share your content. They help you win more audience – how funny!

But Don't Open Your Eyes Too Much...

In marketing, there is a concept called marketing myopia, which involves looking too closely at short term results rather than focusing on long term growth. Sometimes that situation may require you to close your eyes, stop looking at short term analysis, and think about what the bigger picture is.

Some things do not have direct return on investments but can lead to a gain in followers or even capital down the road.

It's all about planning for the future rather than settling for immediate gratification.

The Question You Always Need to Ask Yourself

A loyal audience is the heart to success, and the bigger this audience, the bigger your personal brand. And so you have to be dedicated to growing it, every single day.

But the question is: what type of audience should you aim to build? The more specific your target the audience, the more focused your content can be. And a more focused content is normally of higher quality and much more organized in a way that is appealing to viewers.

In achieving this audience, social platforms and email lists are a great way to have that initial contact. We'll talk about some strategies and tactics later in this book, but they change constantly.

You should be laser focused, and dedicated to building your audience. Whatever it is that you do, this is the only way to really grow. No matter how good you are at what you do, your success depends on it. The question that should be always in your head should be: how do I build my audience?

The Second Question to Always Ask Yourself

The second most important question to ask yourself when building your audience is: "How do I engage my audience?" or "How do I keep this audience warm?"

Imagine that once someone joins your audience, this new fan is cold. You need to engage with this new fan in order to get him or her warm enough to be receptive to your work. And you need to keep it warm. You need to retain this audience.

As a rule of thumb, the warmer your audience is, the more engaged and involved it will be. They will open your emails more. They will like your posts more. They will buy your products more. They will share your content more. They will talk about you with their friends. And so on.

There are multiple of ways to keep an audience warm, which we will talk about in the next couple of pages. But, again, the golden rule is to always ask yourself "How can I keep my audience warm?" and to work accordingly.

Living On the Edge

The best way to grow is to stay on the edge. That's it. No matter what people say, no matter what you think is the truth, you can't grow if you're staying in your comfort zone.

If you follow my Instagram or blog, you'll know that I talk about this a lot.

But this is the cold hard truth. You won't be comfortable building your personal brand. And even less growing it.

Amazon is not profitable year after year. But are they a huge brand? Hell yeah. And even Kanye West. Go ask him if he grew his personal brand by not staying on the edge. He'll answer you that it's all about the edge. He even tweeted that he was 53 million in debt in early 2016. But that's another story.

Every month, I invest almost every dollar of profit I make in growing my personal brand even bigger. I keep myself on the edge so I can grow and profit from it later on. Instead, I could easily go the other way and save more money, or buy better cars and expensive watches.

But growth feels better. Staying on the edge feels not comfortable, but you learn to love it. Because again, growth feels better. And that's how you'll grow your personal brand.

Break the Rules

I've noticed, over the past few years that great marketers tend to find amusement in breaking the rules. They understand that rules are what control us, and what control us makes us less creative. Of course, some rules are made to give us the basics, a starting point from which we can lay a foundation and spring board off. But once we've learnt the bare basic of whatever we're attempting to do – and truly understand those basics inside and out – then it's time to break free.

Once we train our minds to break the rules of marketing, we're able to see the world and the consumer from a fresh new perspective.

We're able to stand out, while everybody follows the same path. And marketing is very dependent on separating yourself from the crowd.

There's a line I love that summarizes pretty much all that was said about being unique. I don't remember who it is from, but might I might as well share it with you: "When everybody goes right, go left."

Don't Be Afraid to Be Controversial

People love controversy. It gets shared, it gets talked about, and it gets awareness.

A lot of people are afraid of being controversial because it's personal.

P.T Barnum – one of the greatest entrepreneur of the 19th century – once said: "There is no such thing as bad publicity." In my opinion, this is 90% of the time true. The more your name gets talked about, the better, even if it means putting yourself in front of the firing squad. The exception to this rule is if your controversy is immoral or illegal. Other than that, don't be afraid of shocking people and doing something unexpected. It will spark conversation and you'll get attention.

For example, the Starbucks red cup campaign created a lot of controversy and offended a portion of the Christian community. But it also boosted Starbucks sales and got people to talk about them. In fact, according to Starbucks, a photo of the red cup was shared every 14 seconds on Instagram.

Controversy will help you get more sales and more awareness to your brand. But are you ready to deal with the pressure is the question you should ask yourself before putting yourself in the center of the flames.

Don't Be Afraid of Hate

This very much goes hand in hand with controversy, and its the simple fact that people who hate you will talk about you. Regardless whether what they say is good or bad, you'll benefit from the mere exposure of having your name go around.

For me personally, when I was doing music, a lot of people were hating me because I was young and had a particular style of music that didn't conform to what the majority wanted content creators to follow. But at the end of the day, it was free publicity for me and all I had to do was continue creating music that I loved.

So at the end of the day, not everyone is going to like you. But if you aim to build a strong personal brand, it means standing out, and standing out entails some criticism.

A Lesson of Content Marketing from Justin Bieber

On January 9th 2007, a mother decided it would be a good idea to upload a video of her son singing on YouTube. She therefore uploaded it under the channel name "Kidrauhl." The video gets massive views due to her son's immense talent alone. They then decide to produce more videos.

Fast forward a couple of years later, her son – Justin Bieber – is one of the biggest pop stars of our generation.

If they would have never uploaded these videos, Justin would have most probably never seen that much success.

However, people didn't discover Justin from an ad. Justin didn't build his audience by sending out flyers.

His brand grew from producing great content and taking time to perfect his craft.

The moral of this story? Content creates brands. Exceptional content breads exceptional, long lasting brands.

You Don't Need a Blog to Blog (Content on Each Social Media)

A lot of people want to start blogging or creating content, but they see the task bigger than what it really is. They think they need to set up a fancy website, and so on, to start the process.

The truth is that every time you tweet, it's content and marketing.

Every time you share a story on Snapchat, it's content and marketing.

Every time you post a photo or an update on Facebook, it's content and marketing.

Every time you post a photo on Instagram, it's content and marketing.

Platforms such as Facebook and Medium are also a great way to extend your content to an audience that would normally

And the great thing about all of these platforms: they are absolutely free to use.

And even if you have a website, you need to create content on social media platforms because right now, that's the place to be in terms of building an audience. So might as well start now.

The take home message: You don't need a blog to blog.

Recycle Content & Cross Promote (And Repost)

One great way to keep the content flowing is by publishing one of your content onto a different platform, or to create something new out of it.

For example, every once in a while I share marketing tips on my Snapchat. If I believe this marketing tip deserves to get more traction, I then upload it onto YouTube. With this, I can advertise both social media platforms while giving content that I believe is exceptional more attention.

Every YouTube video, I turn it into an Instagram video. Every Twitter quote into a Facebook and an Instagram quote.

By doing that, and by making many content pieces with one, I'm able to create engagement on multiple channels and to leverage as much as possible from every piece of content I put out. It's also a way to reach an audience I would be unable to reach out to with only one social media site as my main content hub.

Get People to Talk About You in Blogs & Press & Interviews

I still remember when they wrote about me in the biggest newspaper in Quebec. It was a two-page article about my first best-selling book and about my work as a whole.

The impact was massive and because it was published by a highly regarded newspaper, more and more people started seeing me and my content as credible. No matter how much advertising or attention you seek online, people will only believe it once someone else tells them. And that's the beauty of PR.

I've got interviewed by dozens of blogs in the last few years. I've talked on the radio. Newspapers have talked about me and YouTubers interviewed me for book clubs. The other day, I got mentioned as one of the top 50 influencer on Snapchat, in the world. Every single time. Every, single, time, it grew my brand.

It's always hard to convince people you're the best, but it comes much easier when someone else tells them.

If you seek to build your personal brand, you should be actively seeking interviews, PR opportunities – no matter how small they are. Every time, people will believe it more than yesterday and you'll gain new viewers.

Become a Guest Blogger

Neil Patel, one of today's greatest online marketers, has leveraged the use of guest blogging to build his brand and to be known as an expert.

Guest blogging is simple: you blog on someone else's publication. Whether it is for a prestigious magazine like Entrepreneur Magazine, or just for your friend starting a new blog, it's a win-win.

First of all, it's great for SEO. You build links to your website, as you get a chance to link your profile to your website. Second, you get to gain a new audience and to get attention from a fresh viewership. Even if you win 2 new fans from it, it's a mission accomplished.

Lastly, you're being seen as an expert. If a publication trusted you enough to blog about a specific subject, it means you know what you're talking about! Or at least that's what the Internet is going to think, and it's definitely a boon to your credibility.

Jump on the News! News jacking

Within the last few years, one of the strategies I've used to be recognized as an expert is to profit on important news in the marketing world.

The trick is simple: I'm subscribed to important news regarding the marketing industry and anytime something insightful or interesting comes out, I make sure to blog about it. By doing that, my audience considers me a reliable source for news regarding the marketing realm. And I purposefully do this to put myself in a position where others view me as an expert, raising my credibility and the appeal I would have with both a new and old audience.

And of course this doesn't have to do with just the marketing realm. If you're a finance expert, make sure you blog – or re-post articles – about the most important news. If you're lawyer, it can be about important news in the law industry.

By doing that, your audience will look up to you as the authority and the go-to expert to stay up to date.

By the way, if you don't have a blog yet, it can be as simple as reposting news articles from credible websites to your social pages. So long as you're interacting with and speaking about the important things that are going on in your niche, more and more people will come to you seeking information.

Dress Like a Million Bucks

The first step to a personal brand? The first impression.

And when people meet you for the first time, what is the first thing people look at? Your look.

You have to dress for confidence and certainly dress in the same way you would want your brand to be viewed.

Want to become a Hollywood actor? Dress like that. Want to be the greatest photographer in the country? Picture how that photographer would dress and dress like that.

It doesn't mean you have to spend lots of money on your look. You simply have to brand your look and to always stay clean.

To build a great personal brand, you have to look like a success. So dress like one.

Become a Crazy Scientist (Double Down, Cut)

Marketing yourself is just like marketing a business. You have to stop being dumb and focus on what works. So how do you that? You keep testing thing out. You become obsessed with curiosity and willingness to experiment with paths that may have not been taken before.

Once you've found something that works, you double down on it and cut the rest. This way you save time and energy on working with methods that have shown to work for you.

You can try that with a lot of things related to your personal brand.

Every month, you should try at least 2 new ways to build your audience.

You should try at least 2 new ways to monetize your personal brand.

You should try at least 2 new ways to get people to pay attention to your story.

Once you find something that works – something that pays – stick to it. Just for a while.

Do it Yourself, Stay Independent & Keep the Control

Building a brand is about keeping the control. It's about doing your ideas the way you want.

A few years ago, you had to be signed by a label to release a CD.

You had to sign an impossible-to-get contract to design your clothing line.

You had to get a publishing deal – which was hard to get – to publish your book.

Now, you can do all that without these big corporations controlling your ideas and your brand. And even more than that: the more you keep control and stay independent, the more you can build your personal brand the way you want it. You begin working for yourself rather than working for a higher up. And trust me, by working for yourself your creativity sky rockets.

Go ahead, self publish that book. Self produce that documentary you wished to produce. Design the clothing line you wish all the city would wear.

You don't need anybody else.

Associate Yourself with Influencers (Example Tai Lopez)

In July 2016, I got invited to Tai Lopez's – a famous online marketer and entrepreneur– house, for a social media influencers party. With all the influencers invited, there was a total following of 1 billion people.

Tai was smart for doing that. By associating himself with influencers, and inviting them to his house for an "all included" party, he grew his influence and personal brand big time.

But it's all about using other people's influence to grow yours. This is the best way to grow your brand.

To promote my first best-selling book, The Marketing Blueprint, I decided to turn myself to pages and influencers with millions of fans and paid them to post a photo of them reading my book. I did that for 1 year and my influence grew everyday. Book sales also went through the roof. I'm still doing it as of today just because of how effective that strategy is.

No matter what product you're selling, no matter what craft you have, and no matter what personal brand you want to grow, associating yourself with influencers and using their influence will grow your brand.
Look how politicians use every day celebrities or influencers to endorse them. Look at how authors ask famous people to make a testimonial for their books. Same thing for movie producers.

Use other people's influence to grow yours. Pay them to do it.

It's going to grow your audience and influence.

And though it may take some money in the beginning to embark on this, this initial investment will pay off in greater viewership numbers, bigger sales, and more profit.

Have a Niche, But Let the Masses Know About You

Steve Jobs was in the entrepreneurship niche, but a lot of people outside of this specific realm know about him and were familiar with his mission.

Donald Trump is in the real estate niche, Picasso was in the art niche, Scooter Braun is an artist manager, Oprah Winfrey is a TV personality, Beyonce a singer, David Beckham is a world class athlete, yet we recognize these powerful names despite perhaps not being part of the niche they all reside in.

Even if you're owning a niche, and have a very focused craft, people outside of this niche – the masses – need to know and enjoy what you do. The good news is that every type of work can be enjoyed by the masses if marketed in appropriately. By allowing your brand to have an overarching reach, you are in the prime position in growing your personal brand.

Build your email list by giving away something for free

Email marketing is simple but is extremely powerful. It's still, after all these years, one of the best and most direct way to reach your audience with just a few clicks. Sure you can use social media sites such as Facebook and Snapchat, but policies can change very quickly, to the point where your plan of reaching out to your audience becomes tampered. But email lists are yours and no one can take that power away from you.

I built a 15,000 people email list by giving away free chapters of my book. One of my client in the e-commerce business built a 30,000 email list by giving away prizes. Hubspot, the leading CRM platform once did a campaign where they gave free teddy bears with a QR code to go download an ebook. Needless to say, they all grew their email lists astronomically.

You could give away multiple things to build your email list. It can be free updates, free news, free insights, free tips, free books, free videos, free products, free anything.

As long as it's free and relevant, and you ask for an email subscription, you'll most likely get a decent following.

Oh, and don't forget, you need to get this offer in front of people so you can get their email. So once you've built a landing page with your offer, make sure you send traffic to it.

Have a Road Map

It's probably your first time setting off on this journey and the destination may very well be a mystery, an unknown that you have never crossed into. You may have a vision of how you'll get there, but a vague vision of your efforts is simply not enough. What you need is a well defined road map, a concrete plan of what you're doing and when you're doing it.

Every once in a while, I like to sit down, with a good cup of coffee and music that I love and make sure to put my vision on paper and the steps I need to take to get there. Is this a business plan? Maybe, but not really. Is this a to-do list? Maybe, but not really.

I simply take a sheet of paper and list all the things I want my personal brand to be, I put as much as information as possible so I see it as if it was already true. Then I put as well on this sheet all the steps, achievements, work, people I need to meet, experience I need to make, languages I need to learn, things I need to improve upon, goals I need to reach, skills I need to develop, tasks needed to be done to get there, and so on, to this ultimate vision.

I humbly believe that every person striving to grow their personal brand and become the best in their niche should do it. It not only helps you define your vision, but it also helps to navigate with clarity.

Build and Keep Your Momentum

Marketing is all about momentum.

In my first book, I refer to a brand as a wheel, and the marketplace as a big hill. You need to climb the hill and give it a steady and constant push. But, as you start pushing, the wheel will start to roll and it will get easier and easier to climb. But if you stop, it will slow down and roll back on you.

When building your personal brand, the same concept applies. You need to keep going; stopping may just bring you back to where you started, and all that hard work you put in could go to waste.

This is a pretty huge reason why companies that are initially successful can disappear almost over night. It all has to do with them stopping or becoming too comfortable with their position that they don't put in as much effort as they initially did. If you're committed to your audience and to your brand, you need to keep the momentum alive and in full force.

And trust me: it's much easier to maintain momentum, then to lose it and try to create the buzz again.

Be Consistent – The Mere Exposure Effect

In psychology, there's a phenomenon called the *mere exposure effect*. This phenomenon goes around the principle that humans tend to develop a preference for what they are familiar with, which normally means they are more comfortable with people, places, and even ideas that they are exposed more to.

You can't hope to be seen as an influencer, an authority, a brand, if you're not constantly in front of your audience. The more you get in front of people and show case what you have to offer, the more likely your audience will begin to trust your brand and feel comfortable interacting with your brand.

In the last chapter, I talk about this around the principle of the "momentum". But here I'll simply sum it up as: consistency. Being consistent when it comes to presenting yourself to your audience is key to success.

Answer Every Email (Stay Close to Your Audience)

When I didn't have a budget, I was building my audience one by one, a single relation at a time. At the end of the day however, you're not just focusing on a few relationships here and there. Rather, It's thousands of one-on-one relationships that need to be nurtured.

That's why I believe every human behind a personal brand should strive to answer and communicate one-on-one as much as possible with people in their audience. Interacting with the people who have gotten behind your brand or are even showing a tiny morsel of interest deserve some of your attention.

So answer emails your fans send you.

Answer viewers' comments once in a while.

Like photos from your followers

Send thank you's.

Follow your most loyal followers.

Strive to do these things even if you have too many followers, because even a simple comment or a like might be the difference between losing a fan in 15 weeks or having him stay for the next 15 years.

Google Yourself Everyday

"Your brand is what people say when you're not in the room."
-   Jeff Bezos, Amazon CEO

I probably Google my name every single day. And you should too.

The advantage of this goes back to the idea of collecting information. You want to be save as to how people are reacting to you and your brand, and thereby helping you shift your focus as the situation requires. In this respect, it amazes me how many people building a brand don't even know what people say online about them.

Taking a few minutes to Google yourself can bring a host of important information such as:

-   What people are saying about you
-   Relevant news and blog posts about you
-   Reviews about your products

Then, once you find something about you on Google, it is an opportunity for you to gather information, feedback, and data to help you grow. It is also an opportunity for you to interact and engage with an audience, regardless if the information is positive or negative.

It's time to Google yourself.

You'll Need Mentors

I still remember that call. I was so nervous. But who was on the other line? Leonard Riggio, the CEO and founder of Barnes & Nobles.

See, I've always had this thing to learn from people who've done it, who've made it in their industry. People who've built successful businesses, but mostly people who've built personal brands. Today, a lot of people talk about the importance of mentors. But they forget to mention that you can have multiple mentors. You're not tied to one.

When building a personal brand, gathering as much advice as possible will help you grow and avoid some common mistakes. It will help you see more clearly when your vision gets blurred.

So back to Leonard Riggio… How did I get this call? I simply emailed his assistant. Same thing happened when I got on a call with Walmart Canada's chief marketing officer.

Brian Grazer, the movie producer behind Splash and American Gangster, calls these "curiosity conversations." Since the beginning of his career, he invited all types of people – from the richest man in the world to astrophysicists – for lunch. In his book, A Curious Mind, he shows us that meeting and learning from all types of people helped him grow his craft and his career so much.

My advice to you would be: email 10 people today that already built a successful personal brand. Invite them for lunch. Or get on a call with them.

Everybody has something to teach you. And the knowledge you learn from these people will be invaluable to your experience and your mission of growing your own brand.

You'll Need Books

If you want to become the best at what you do, you have to read what you need to read to become the best at what you do.

I probably read 2 books per week. Some times more.

When Warren Buffet was once asked what were the keys to success, he pointed at a pile of books near him. It's reported that he reads for about 80% of his day, coming in as no surprise as to how absolutely intellectually gifted he is.

Bill Gates similarly reads about 1 book per week. Mark Cuban reads 3 hours per day. Elon Musk told reporters one time that he learned to build rockets by reading book.

Oprah Winfrey is an avid reader, so is Mark Zuckerberg.

You get my point: The world's most successful people are readers and constantly hungry for new information to learn from. This relates to finding a mentor, except this time, you can lean from these mentors right in the comfort of your own home.

But don't be afraid. It doesn't mean that you have to read 500 pages per day. It can be as simple as one chapter every morning, or every night. The goal here is to simply read every single day to keep learning and to keep sharpening your axe.

Keep learning, keep reading, and your craft will get better.

PART 3 – Money talk.

The only way monetization can happen

Having a personal brand is the only way to monetize that brand. Too many people try to monetize their brand too early or too often, without effectively thinking of a plan in achieving their goal. By doing so, they don't leverage the power of building their brand and they don't grow as quickly.

I like to think of myself the brand-building process as a drug cartel: the only way to make money is to increase the demand from a consumer base. But to do that, you have to effectively take time and energy in planning and organizing that brand and its mission. Only then will you see results and profits.

If you can't leverage your personal brand, it's not worth shit.

Now, yes, you need a well established personal brand. We understand that. But here's the thing: if you can't leverage it, if you can't monetize it, it isn't worth shit. Sorry for these big words, but it's the cold, hard truth.

To make it worth your while, you need to actively take strides in earning profit and new contacts for your personal brand to increase the revenue of any currently held activities.

The next few pages will help you understand the concept of personal brand monetization, and a few avenues you could take to achieve that purpose.

Keep It Simple

Personal brands do not require complex strategies or multiple income streams to make your brand a success. They think they have to set up ads, create a complete membership zone on their website, or even write a book. All these things are beneficial, but most of the time, they are overwhelming for followers and ultimately leads to a decrease in followership.

The general rule is that the more complicated you make your strategies, the less focused or clear your resulting message will be.

In my case, I monetize my personal brand in only two ways: marketing projects and books, at this current moment anyways. Of course, I will probably go further one day, maybe even during the time you pick up this book. But for now, I try to highlight these two aspects as perfectly as possible.

One way I like to see it is in terms of "craft and scale." For the craft, ask yourself: how can I monetize with my specific craft or talent. In my instance, it is through marketing services and projects. For the scale part, ask yourself: how can I scale my revenue, without working more hours. In my instance, it is through books.

If you can have these two things, things will go well.

Where I Come From, Money is Bad. Here's the Truth.

Where I come from – maybe where you come from too – money is evil. But here's the truth: generating revenue is the only way to actualize your dreams in the world. Generating revenue is the best sign of respect you can give to your talents.

It allows you to do what you love while being able to live comfortably. It allows you to give back. It allows you to take on bigger projects. It allows you to achieve your dreams and run with them to do bigger and better things everyday.

Taking Advantage of Your Personal Brand for Opportunities

When we hear personal brand monetization, we think about money. But your brand is so much more than just the money.

You can leverage your personal brand by using it to get more opportunities such as:

· Better job opportunities.
· Getting invited at better networking events.
· Getting on calls with top mentors in your industry.
· Getting whatever you want to get.
· Getting more demand for your current business.

That being said, I could make the list longer, like getting better treatment at the restaurant. But I'm sure you get the point, and I'll let your mind wander.

My point is simple: every single day, you need to be asking yourself how you can leverage your hardly built personal brand. Every time you need something, every time you have an opportunity or a dream you want to achieve, make sure you leverage your personal brand. It'll help you with whatever you do.

Charge Them for Your Skills (Consulting)

The simplest way and most effective way to monetize your personal brand is through consulting and freelancing.

Remember in part 1 when we discussed about having a craft? Well, here comes the time you monetize it.

If you're a chef, get people to hire you to cook. Put your culinary services on your website.

If you're a graphic designer, get people to hire you to design logos, website, or any kind of graphic design.

If you're a good writer, get people to hire you to write for them. It could be books, movies, brochures, slogans, or anything that requires well written writing.

Consulting and freelancing requires small investments to start making money and you have the chance to do what you love and what you're good at.

Tap into your talents. Charge for it.

They Want a Product!

At the beginning of this chapter, I talked about scale. This is where it happens. Monetizing your personal brand through services and freelancing is great, but you mostly trade time for money. It has its limit.

When you build your personal brand, you are able to build a large following. Let's imagine that you built a 100,000 following on Instagram. Will every single one of these followers inquire your services? Probably not. Even if they did, that number of inquiries would be greatly overwhelming.

That's when building a product comes in. Building a product gives you the chances to solve a need and bring a solution to your audience, without trading time for money. Once you've built the product, you can sell repeatedly and with efficiency.

If you're a designer, you could write a book about your best design practices, or you could sell Photoshop tools that help your audience with their graphic designs.

If you're a dancer, you could sell video dance lessons through your website, or even design your own dancing clothes and merchandise.

The question ultimately leads to what your brand represents and what product or service you are going to build.

Endorsements

Endorsements are an even simpler way to make money with your personal brand.

The premise is simple: Companies pay you to associate your name with their products and brand (and sometime promote it). It can go from simply associating your name with it in advertisements, to hosting their events, all the way to posting on your social media pages about their products. It can also go all the way up to licensing your name to them, while they build the product around it. For instance, a wide variety of celebrities and social media personalities do that with perfume fragrances or differing types of merchandise.

Every day, I get offers from social media influencers, athletes, and movie stars asking me to pay them to promote my products. Sometimes it fits my current projects or client projects, sometimes it doesn't.

Closing endorsements deals is a great way to monetize your influence once your following gets bigger.

Speaking Engagements

Every once in a while, I get emails from companies or organizations that want me to come and hold a keynote. I can charge up to thousands of dollars for a 45-minute conference.

Needless to say, organizing and giving such a presentation can take a lot of time, but is definitely worth the effort. It's a great opportunity for monetization, but also to share insight, converse with an audience that may already be interested in your niche, and even to have an initial contact with a new audience that you could potentially convert to your brand.

However, not all speaking engagements come in the same shape or form. Some can be in the form of a workshop, as a live interview, or as a simple keynote presentation directed to various different audiences each time. But one thing stays the same: you are able to exert your brand on an audience that you may not have been able to do otherwise.

Never Discount Your Value.

Regardless of where you stand in promoting your brand and gaining a followership, one thing always stays the same: Never. Discount. Your. Brand.

Have you ever seen Louis Vuitton letting a purse go at 60%, or Justin Bieber hosting a free show? Of course not, because if they did, they wouldn't be where they are today.

When providing a service or a brand, regardless of what it may be, know your worth and stick to it. By holding your brand at high value, your following will do the same; and that is key for growing and maintaining a successful brand.

THANK YOU!

At the End of the Day, You're Only as Good as Your Work

This book is about personal brand, and how to build it. The tips you've learnt in this book will help you tremendously to grow your brand, but let me be clear on one thing: it will never replace doing exceptional, long-term work.

Rolex built its brand by making elegant and beautiful watches.

Michael Jackson built its brand by being a phenomenal and stunning dancer.

Michael Jordan by being a world-class basketball player.

And Richard Branson by constructing some of the biggest and most successful companies in the world.

That being said, if we all strive to become the greatest of our generation, we need to focus on doing great work. That's really how we can grow.

Nothing can replace this.

Let's do great work.

Be Like Lil Dicky

As you probably know, I love rap music. One of the hottest rappers right now is David Burd, also known as Lil Dicky.

As funny as his name is, his story is exceptionally inspiring. Prior to being one of the hottest hip hop artists right now, David was a copywriter in an ad agency. When he decided it was time to become a rapper, a lot of people were doubting him. How could you change from working in an advertising agency to become a rapper? What a dream!
Be he kept going.

But he let no one define who he was going to be.

You're the only one who should define yourself.

You're the only one who should know when it's time to reinvent yourself.

Be the master of your brand.

Be the master of YOU.

Work So You Win in 20 Years.

Talking about reinventing yourself, we should always work in order to win the long game.

What's good today might not be good tomorrow.

Reinvent yourself every single day.

Reinvent the way you work.

Reinvent the way you market yourself.

If you see something you'd like to do, do it.

If you see a new platform that might help your personal brand, jump on it!

Try a lot of things.

Test.

Fail.

Win.

Choose the long term growth over the short term glory.

Lose some battles, but ultimately win the war.

Play the long game.

Building a brand is about thinking at a 20-30 years' scale.

Maybe 100 years.

Or 200.

At the end of the day, all that matters is that you enjoy the ride, take your time, and make the fun last.

There's always something ahead. So Look up to it.

Thank you

Yes…

We've come to the end of this short book. I'm glad you stayed and learned some valuable advice to help you steer onto the path of success.

I want to thank you for grabbing this book. It truly means a lot to me.

If you'd like to learn more about my current projects, hire me for your brand, or read some of my free blog posts, check out my website at www.julesmarcoux.com

From the bottom of my heart: Thank You